1

5 Steps to Homecoming

Dr. Anthony J. Albright

7 January 2020

Preface

On September 11, 2001, I was prepared to attend classes at The Evergreen State College. I had enrolled, established financial aid, and would be pursuing a degree in secondary education. I was 18 years old and ready to take on the world. That morning, my life would change forever as I watched the attacks on New York and elsewhere unfold on the news. I never went to class that day. I never attended Evergreen. Instead on September 18, 2001, I walked into my Army recruiter's office near Fuller's Market in Centralia, WA and took the oath of enlistment.

From that time, until March 17, 2005, I did everything the Army told me to do. When they told me to jump, I didn't ask how high, I jumped as high and long as I could. I let it soak in. I became what they wanted me to be, a faster, stronger, more violent version of myself. I was high speed, low drag,

Airborne, all the way. I went places and did things I never thought I could. I performed physical feats I never imagined. I was fundamentally changed.

I had become highly capable of adapting to new situations. I could act with a quickness. I could run for hours. I was confident in my abilities to do anything. I saw challenges as mere obstacles to overcome. I had training that could be relied upon to guide my decisions and capable leaders when that training failed. It seemed like the rest of life would be smooth sailing: like no challenge could possibly ever stand in my way again.

In the aftermath of my service, my marriage fell apart. I had trouble finding good work. I was behind. I became homeless. I was depressed and ashamed and for a period of 3-4 years, I felt totally lost. It was like nothing I had done when I was in the Army made any difference at all. Nobody cared; I was like this antiquated person with strange ways and a bad temper who had no place in the society where I once called home. My friends had moved on. My family didn't know who I was anymore.

It was as if I had gone to a party that had been going on for the last 4 years without me. I was in completely the wrong clothing. I didn't know what anyone was talking about. I hadn't been there for any of the conversations and I'd never heard the music that was playing. The faces in the crowd were familiar, but they spoke a different language.

It wasn't until I made the decision to move to Minnesota and return to school that I really began to regain some feeling of community: some sense of belonging. In college, the military was something I did, but it wasn't who I was. I'm thankful for that because they didn't seem to appreciate when my military self would appear. I could be hostile, domineering, and inconsiderate. I was lucky I had access to different sides of my personality. Without them, I fear I would have been even more lost than I was.

I succeeded in school by learning to adapt to my new surroundings. People didn't care that I was confident, only that I was competent. My words meant far less and my actions meant far more than I was used to. People felt like they couldn't know me until I was vulnerable around them. I had to be open an honest about things that they really had no need or right to know. Those times when I disclosed information about myself that was humiliating were the times when I was most successful in building relationships that pulled me back into community.

Fast forward to today. I've completed a doctoral degree; the feelings I have inside are utterly indescribable. I should not be here. So many of my sisters and brothers in arms are not here. It is with them in mind that I dedicate my efforts going forward to improving the lives of those who transition out of the military and attempting to help them build bridges back to their communities.

Step 1: Basic separates from our support networks. We need to reestablish them.

If you joined when I did, you remember the pay phone line at Basic Training. You got 5 minutes per soldier if you were lucky, and the drill sergeant had his finger on the receiver while you called Mom, told her you were okay, you loved her, and you would be busy for the next few weeks, and then hung up. Some of you went to Ft. Jackson and got more time. Some of you had cell phones and didn't have to go through the pain of entering the phone card number you got from the PX on your one shopping trip before Basic Training, in which you bought everything you were told to and charged it to your first month's pay.

Some of you might remember bidding your family farewell and flying off on a plane or boarding a bus, maybe for the first time, to go to an unfamiliar place and do extraordinary things. Maybe your proud dad dropped you off. Maybe it was the mom who didn't agree with your choice. Maybe the police department dropped you off. Maybe it was your recruiter. Maybe you didn't have anyone there. You probably met 2-3 other young people at the airport or bus stop and one of you was put in charge of the folder, your first duty assignment.

Maybe you had a fight before you left. Maybe you sold or gave away things. Maybe you broke up with someone. Maybe someone promised to wait. Maybe you left after your marriage. Maybe you were running from something. Maybe you were running toward something. Maybe you were rising above your station. Maybe you climbing out of poverty. Maybe you were disowned for joining. Maybe you were honored. Maybe your picture went up on someone's wall. Maybe it was taken down.

Under whatever circumstances you left, you left behind a world as you knew it. You left behind your parents or your significant other. You left behind your friends and your job. You left behind local politics and the homeowner's association complaining about the length of the grass. Maybe you left behind a child or a spouse. Maybe you left behind welfare or desperation. Maybe you left behind an addiction or a gang.

Whatever you left behind, you left what felt like home and you went somewhere else. You went to another time, another place, another home, another family, and you grew another face. You grew a war face. You hardened. You got close to your siblings in arms. Your successes were publicly celebrated; for your defeats, you were publicly chastised. All the while, you grew more and more like a soldier. You left behind the person whose life you lived before. You opened the door to something greater, to be something more. But in doing so, you closed the door on childish or innocent things, leaving them behind, unwanted and unneeded.

There were many different reasons to join. Some of you, like me, joined at a time when something extraordinary was happening and you couldn't help but volunteer or else consider yourself less of a patriot. Some of you joined to get college paid for (good luck navigating that process). Some of you joined for medical benefits or for a middle-class job. Whatever made you join, it was a disruptive event in your life. There is a life before the military and a life after the military and you know the difference. Some of us will forever separate ourselves into three personalities (before, during, after).

Over the course of this chapter, we'll explore those three phases and what changes between them. We'll look at who joins the military and why. We'll look at what happens to you during your service, and we'll look at what happens after your service, both in the immediate aftermath and a few years down the road. As we do, I want you to consider what part of that process has the largest influence over who you are today. Are you more like you were before the military? Do you still feel like you're a part of active military culture? Do you feel like you're in some kind of post-military state? Let's dig deeper.

Self Work

Are you most like you were before the military, during, or after today? If you're still in the military, do you feel like you can ever become who you used to be? Do you want to?

_____
_____
_____
_____
_____

Do you feel like you're still a part of military culture?

_____
_____
_____
_____
_____

Do you feel like you're in some sort of post-military state, but not quite like you were before or during your service?

_____

_____

_____

_____

_____

Let's Dig Deeper: Describe who you are today and what has had the greatest influence on your life.

_____

_____

_____

_____

_____

_____

_____

_____

_____

_____

Before

My family wasn't always poor. We owned a piece of land out in the country and had a trailer on it, so we were pretty much on-par with most of the families in the area. It wasn't a ritzy place, but we got by and our family was close. My dad was gone for most of my life and Mom did her best, but she was over-worked and underpaid.

My school didn't have much in the way of an arts program. The math teacher and English teacher would sometimes get together and offer a reading of a classical Greek or Renaissance play. Football and basketball were far more important than such things. Even the band only really existed so that they could play at the games. Let me tell you, when a team made it to state, the whole town would shut down and go root for those athletes, but we couldn't fill half the gym for the talent show.

When Dad was around, we used to travel as a gospel singing group, sort of like the Partridge Family. Dad would preach, he and Mom would sing, my oldest brother ran sound and my middle brother played the drums. If there was time, I would come up and sing a song from the Psalty Songbook collection. It was an idyllic time in my life. I developed a love for performing, and that love followed me for a long time, even after Dad was gone.

Growing up as a performer in the country wasn't a great way to be well-liked. It would have been one thing if I was also charismatic, but I couldn't rise above the depression over what I lost when Dad was gone. People weren't sure what to think of me. They would question whether or not I was gay. They would try to make me angry, because it was really easy to do. They would make fun of me for not having the newest clothes or the best brands.

I'll remember until my dying day coming into school really proud to be wearing Jordan's that my mom got from the thrift store. Someone had colored over the ugly color they came in with a dark blue marker, and I was super proud of them, even if they were a little worn out. I proudly told all my friends at school about them but was met with skepticism. The Air Jordan logo had faded and one of the kids (I think maliciously) read the side and said, "Air Jordache." I was gutted. I never bragged about the shoes again. I hated them after that. I still had to wear them because my mom spent money and effort trying to get me what I wanted in the only way she could afford to do it. It wasn't her fault the kids were cruel, just like it wasn't her fault she couldn't afford better.

Getting out of that place was never a question in my mind. I knew I had to. I just didn't know how to accomplish it. Still, I was sure that my time would come.

In junior high I met a girl and we started dating. Soon, we were planning how our lives would go. I started working at the local Wal-Mart and saving for a ring to ask her to marry me, but soon I figured out it would never happen on that wage, at least not like I wanted it to. I toyed with the idea of college. I even got accepted, which was difficult for me to believe -- my grades weren't great.

Then September 11th happened. It took a week for me to stew on it, but soon, both me and my girlfriend had decided that the best way for us to help was to join the Army. We knew it would get us out of our little town, but most of all, we knew that we couldn't live with ourselves if we didn't answer the call when it was coming so clearly. We went to the recruiter and he was only too happy to take us both on the spot. We went to MEPS that Friday and by November, I was on my way to Ft. Sill, OK.

Before we left, we sold my car and bought bags with a few things we thought we might need: socks and running shoes, toiletries. We bought all of the things we could before we left, not knowing that we would basically have to throw it all away when we got there.

My separation from family was already underway when I left. No one dropped me off at the airport to go to Ft. Sill for Basic Training. Mom was gone with her latest boyfriend. I was having trouble communicating with my dad. My girlfriend's mom was quite angry we were joining and would have to wait awhile to see her daughter off in January anyway. My church had basically thrown me out, along with my mom, for being part of a "broken home." I felt like I was throwing a lit match over my shoulder as I left, and in a lot of ways, that was true. I didn't feel connected then, but little did I know how disconnected I could become.

Self Work

What/who did you leave behind when you left for the military?

_____

_____

_____

_____

_____

_____

_____

_____

_____

_____

_____

_____

_____

During

It was hard to be first to leave. I knew that my girlfriend would be headed to Ft. Leonard Wood later on, but she was always the more capable one. It had always been the plan for her to join. For me, this was a reaction to what had happened. I was retaliating with everything I had, which was essentially my life. So, each morning as we ran like we had never run, endured monotony, and embraced the suck, I thought of the attacks on New York, and I about how proud my lady back home would be. And I ran. I ran fast. I toed the line right away. I stood tall. I was proud to serve.

November in Ft. Sill isn't a lot of fun. There were mornings where there was sheet ice just covering the roads. Surely, I thought, we wouldn't try to run on that. But run we did, and if you fell, you got smoked for falling out. A constant line-drive wind blew over the range for BRM, making the cement fox holes wail like half-full soda bottles; the drill sergeants "accidentally" kicked extra rounds into the fox hole because they didn't want to be there any longer than they had to be. We crawled around in what was supposed to be wet mud and rappelled onto sand that should have been absorbent but likely would have broken something if you had the bad luck to fall.

When I was at AIT, the news came from Ft. Leonard Wood that my lady had washed out of Basic and wasn't going to continue. This cleared my eyes even more as to the importance of my mission. I knew I had to succeed: I was carrying both of us now. I went through AIT processing at Ft. Lee, then to Airborne Orientation Course, then to Airborne, then back to Lee for Rigger School. It was a lot of training, but by the end, I was fit and ready to fight. I knew everything I needed to know. I wanted to deploy. I was hungry for it. I have to say, I didn't really know what I was hungry for.

Life on base as a "permanent party" felt strange to me. My job was just a job. If I worked fast, I could go home early. I often did. There was enough downtime. It was easy to get a bit out of shape and revert back to old habits. Even so, warning orders came and we responded. There were moments of action and moments of waiting. There was monotony and there was fun. There was ritual and ceremony and all manner of ways in which you could feel important.

I still remember when I first received a mobilization warning order. It was in the middle of the night and I got a phone call. It woke my wife up. I received my instructions about where to report and by what time and was told I was to proceed with all speed and not stop. I got into my car and drove to the base in the dark. I can't remember what was on the radio, only that it was on. The normally busy streets of Tacoma, WA seemed deserted and it seemed like I alone was driving to the base. When I got to the freeway exit I found a long line of cars waiting to get through the civilian security checkpoint. Civilian gate security was always so uptight. They were like mall cops but with less to do. I rolled through the gate and to the airfield, parked, left my keys with a squad mate who was staying behind, and boarded a C-17 for my destination. Anywhere in the world in 18 hours seemed like a boast before that.

There was also a sort of impermanence to it all. We never felt settled. There was a promotion to strive for or a transfer we wanted. There was a new school or a deployment or a volunteer-for-something-without-knowing kind of thing. Some people you could tell would be there for life. Some people were there until the moment they could retire. Still others, you thought, maybe they'd be around for a second enlistment. Then there were the people who made you think: how did you make it through basic?

There were a few types of soldier everyone knew. There was at least one E-4 over 30 who just didn't want to be an NCO. There was the soldier who was always on profile. There was the one who took their stripes really seriously and let everyone know about it. There was the one who came in drunk every day and sweated out the booze each morning. There was the chain-smoker who was still faster than you in the two-mile run. There were probably several people you never saw without a dip in their lip. You were quite the motley crew, and yet, you knew each other in ways that transcended all these things. You were siblings in arms, friends, rivals, colleagues, and something more.

Occasionally, something you did while you were in would change you. It wouldn't necessarily be something you noticed on

your own. Maybe you gained a little weight.
Maybe you started having nightmares.
Maybe your E-7 started heaping new tasks
on you and grooming you for NCO work.
Maybe you began to think you weren't cut
out for it. Whatever it was, we all went
through some experience that changed us
fundamentally. For a lot of us it was as
simple as joining and going to Basic. That
was more trauma than some of us had ever
experienced.

Whatever it was, when it happened, you
secretly wondered if you would ever go
back to "normal."

We're all aware of how soldiers are seen.
People assume we have PTSD. Some
assume we're dangerous. Many assume
we're all dangerous, regardless of our jobs.
Being aware of this made us think, "Maybe
there's something to the stereotype." We
began to wonder if we were experiencing or
had experienced the event that would

change us. Maybe we excused it, saying, "Well, of course we changed. We had to be ready to fight a war." But how many of us really did fight a war? How many people in uniform shot at us? For most of us, the answer is none, and yet, we are changed. That much is undeniable.

For me, I was twenty-three years old, with high blood pressure, two kids, a crumbling marriage, and a temper that stemmed from I don't know where. I had back problems from jumping out of too many planes. I would soon gain a hundred pounds. I was totally without a direction as to where to move on from there. I had earned my national defense medal and a few honors. What I left behind in those short few years, though, was something that would take a long time to recover.

Self Work

In which ways did you fight a war?

_____
_____
_____
_____
_____

In which ways did you not?

_____
_____
_____
_____
_____

Were you prepared for the war you fought?

_____
_____
_____
_____
_____

After

We've all heard the myths about leaving the military. When you get out, you get free college and free healthcare. If you have a bad discharge, it'll be upgraded in 6 months. Your country will be proud. Your hometown will throw you a parade. You can come home and run for mayor! Your spouse has been waiting, your kids never grew up and your WW2 veteran grandpa is waiting in your driveway at the position of attention to salute your motorcade as you go by. Hopefully none of you are expecting any of these myths to yet come true.

The reality is, most veterans, cut off from their social support networks, divorced, maybe in a custody battle for kids, having not seen friends in 4 or more years, and broke disappear back into their communities with little to no pomp or recognition, only to find that the world did not stop spinning while they were away. Maybe your favorite restaurant closed.

Maybe your high school merged with a rival high school down the road and you're now called the Ducks for some stupid reason. Maybe there's graffiti on the bench you built for your Eagle Scout project. Maybe there's trash all over the neighborhood. Maybe people are unkind, and nobody seems to acknowledge you. It often becomes quite plain that the community, in some way, didn't need you and if you decide to insert yourself, you're going to have to prove yourself all over again. There is no credit for growing up here. You left. Now you're a stranger.

For an unfortunately high number of veterans, that's enough to end it. They don't want to feel like a spare part in a world that left them behind. So, they check out, whether by abusing drugs or alcohol to numb the pain or by taking a shorter route to death. And unfortunately, the one thing all veterans are familiar with is lethal force. We don't often fail if we decide to end it.

Self Work

Be honest with yourself. Have you ever felt like you would never fit in again back home?

_____
_____
_____
_____
_____

Have you ever felt so alone you felt like people would be better off without you around?

_____
_____
_____
_____
_____

Have you ever thought about killing
yourself?

_____

_____

_____

_____

_____

Interrupting the Downward Spiral

What we have to do over the course of our
re-entry is to slowly reverse and unravel
these things that have been so well-
ingrained over the course of our service.
We have to reconnect with friends and
family. We have to find reasons to care for
our community again. We have to find a
reason, a purpose for living and find people
who won't let us give up on that.

Everyone's story of how they became a
soldier is different. We came from
everywhere. We left many different things.
We joined for all kinds of reasons. We

served in all kinds of different capacities. We experienced all kinds of different things and when we end our service, without a group to hold us accountable and lift us up, we're all equally invisible and alone. What hurts the worst is the duality of not wanting to be praised for our service but wanting to be honored for the aspects of our character that made us willing to serve.

One of the biggest problems, unfortunately, is that when we get out of the military we often feel like other veterans are the only ones who truly get us. Maybe you've got some battle buddies at home, of your generation or another. If so, you'll probably be okay. If not, though, who are you going to? The VFW? The Legion? The Eagles? Who wants to hang out where your grandpa did? Not me. Very few of these organizations appeal to younger vets in any real way. We're white-knuckling it, and it shows.

The biggest organizations for young vets are things like Wounded Warrior Project and DAV, and these focus not on what we can still do for our communities but what is wrong with us, and how much the public should pity us. I've never yet met a veteran who wanted the pity of a civilian. What's worse: they go around raising all kinds of money for God knows what, yet I've never gotten my "feel sorry for your local vet" check. Have you?

Instead, like the invisible minority we are, we disappear into a web of the occasional vet program, free meals on Veteran's Day, and a burial flag that some of our friends and neighbors are surprised by. That's all that becomes of our life-altering sacrifice, all that remains of the person we were for 2-30 years. It becomes a downward spiral from which some of us never escape.

To interrupt the spiral, we have to do four things:

1. Talk to young vets/recruits about the military.
2. Talk to young people about the military before they become recruits/vets.
3. Open up to a close circle of friends about everything.
4. Answer the tough questions and educate people about why they're tough.

Talk to young vets/recruits about the military

We all have these kids in our hometowns. We all see them come and go. A new kid comes to church in ACUs and we know. Someone is doing hometown recruiting at the local fair. We know. Someone has a horrible haircut. We can tell where they've been.

I'm not telling you to run up to some kid and tell him stories about loading body parts on a cargo net back in Nam. I will tell you, though, that being real about what the military is and what it changes about you will do you both some good.

These kids think they're going to storm a German machine gun nest or sail around the world. They think they'll be going to nice places. And they have believed everything the recruiter has told them. Take the opportunity to set the record straight.

Maybe you're thinking, "okay, but where would I go to talk to young people?" If you're totally alone in the world, without family or friends, you can insert yourself in volunteer organizations, like churches, youth sports, high school booster clubs, PTAs, school boards, scouts, and all manner of other organizations. If you're not all alone, that's great, because the place where you can have the greatest impact is in your family and existing social groups. Be the go-to veteran. It doesn't take a lot of effort to lead with some of your stories and prompt questions. Be willing to be that person.

Self Work

What do you wish someone had told you when you first entered the military?

_____

_____

_____

_____

_____

Talk to young people about the military before they become recruits/vets

Young people can be a great audience. In some cases, you might be the first veteran they have spoken to. You have the opportunity to set a tone with them and be their example of what a veteran is.

You could use it to tell the ridiculous stories we all have of the idiotic things our drill sergeants made us do. You could use it to set a serious tone about sacrifice and duty.

You could use it to tell a cautionary tale against the evils of the military-industrial complex. However you choose to present the military to young people will be infinitely more valuable coming from you than it would be coming from a movie or a recruiter. Tell your authentic stories. Share your authentic experience. Be the person you wished you had spoken to before you joined.

Self Work

What truths could you tell a young person who was thinking about joining the military?

_____
_____
_____
_____
_____
_____

Who have you told these truths to?

_____
_____
_____
_____
_____

Why or why not?

_____
_____
_____
_____

Open up to a close circle of friends about everything

This is one of the hardest ones, and one of the areas in which the vets with battle buddies in their area have a leg up. You need to choose some trustworthy people, as soon as possible, and confide in them.

These are not necessarily people you already know. They can be people you meet in the strangest of ways, if you're open to it. One of the people I meet with on a regular basis is someone I met in a Build-a-Bear workshop, when we were both building stuffed animals for foster kids as a part of a charity function through my church.

Choose relationships you know you can invest in. Do trips together. Get a drink together. Meet regularly, whether virtually or in person. Share together, pray together, take up a collection when one of you needs it. Do all of the things that you would have done in a good squad or platoon. Hold each other accountable. And when you feel lost or alone, lean on these people.

My pastor, Peter Haas, calls these groups S.P.A.C.E. groups. The acronym stands for **S**ame Gender, **P**rayer, **A**ccountability, **C**onfession, **E**qual Passion. You can read about them more in his book *Church in Space*.[1]

I can't tell you how important this is. A lot of us end up just a couple hundred dollars away from suicide when we get out. How much better would it be to say to your group of accountability buddies that you need $200 to make rent than to try to make up for a deficit by selling your Jack Daniels bottle collection? Get your SPACE group set up. Get into the weeds with a group of

---

[1] https://www.peterhaas.org/get-a-free-copy-of-my-mini-book-church-in-space-the-secret-to-launching-your-spirituality-to-the-moon/

same-gender people who you can pray
with, stay accountable with, confess to, and
who have equal passion for your faith, or
your hobbies, or something that you do
through which you can relate.

Self Work

List the names of 5 same-gender people you might be able to include in your SPACE group. Make sure these are people you can invest in and people who can afford to invest in you. Find people you can admire but it shouldn't be all people on a pedestal. Find people whose strengths compliment your own, but are different from yours. If you don't have 5, list as many as you have and get to work filling out the rest as soon as you're able.

1. _____
2. _____
3. _____
4. _____
5. _____

Answer the tough questions and educate
people about why they're tough

Did you ever kill anyone? You WILL get
asked this question, someday, by someone,
who thinks they're close enough or privy
enough or cool enough to take your
answer. Chances are, the answer is no, but
it could be yes. Worse yet, maybe you don't
know. Lots of fire takes place from a
distance. Has a sailor on a ship launching
cruise missiles ever killed someone? Who
knows. Has a helicopter crew chief ever
killed someone? Who knows. Hopefully
your parachute rigger never killed anyone,
but who's to know? It's a really complicated
question.

Then there's the next layer of complication.
Maybe you volunteered for the military to
go kill bad guys and you ended up as a 92
series. There's nothing wrong with being a
92 series -- Fort Lee is a beautiful post. But
you've probably got some guilt if you joined

up to kill bad guys and ended up as a quartermaster.

When someone asks if you ever killed someone, they might be triggering your survivor's guilt. They might be asking you to remember a buddy from Basic who ended up an Airborne Ranger and went all over the world sacrificing life and limb until the odds finally caught up to him and this idiot before you wants to ask if you, the quartermaster, ever killed anyone?

Avoid the temptation to ask *them* if they have ever killed anyone. Be calm. Explain to them that most veterans never see combat. If you're comfortable, share an anecdote or two about your service. Explain why this is a complicated question that might have really bad effects on a person either asking or answering it. Warn them not to ask it again. Then drive on.

There will be tough questions. People don't serve in anywhere near the proportion of the population that used to -- the census bureau currently puts it at about 7% of the adult population.[2] Is it any wonder that people are curious? Is it any wonder that they're insensitive? They don't know what they don't know. Educate them like only you can.

---

[2]

https://www.census.gov/library/publications/2020/demo/acs-43.html

Self Work

What is the least comfortable question you've been asked about your service?

_____

_____

_____

What could you tell someone who asked you a difficult question about your service?

_____

_____

_____

Step 2: Living in the military made us speak like the military speaks. We need to pick five party stories and translate them for civilians.

Have you ever noticed the way you speak to people when you know they were in the military? I was antiquing recently with my significant other and I noticed a guy who looked about "Desert Storm" age wearing a hat with the unit patch for the 82nd Airborne on it. I said to him, "Hey Airborne, you serve at Bragg?"

He responded, "Eighty-Deuce through and through. 11 bang bang."

I nodded, "Rigger with 1st Group."

He asked, "Lewis?"

I nodded.

All of this took place within a matter of a few seconds while my partner looked on, wondering what the heck I was talking about and why I was talking to this stranger.

Many of us have had these encounters even before leaving the military. We see a person with a funny haircut in the airport and flip our chins at them. Maybe we wear a pin or a patch or just have that look about us. We'll sit down and they'll use a key term, part of a code, that when sprinkled into a conversation reveals whether this person is what we expect they are, or if our radars are just broken. The things we might say range from something simple like, "You serve?" to something more complex/coded like "Seme pas luces" (Pinelandish for guard all fires). (For the record, I've only ever had one person speak Pinelandish to me and it was when I was wearing the SF crest on my hat.)

English has many dialects. People in England speak differently than people in Georgia, and they both speak differently from people speaking English in India. Still, in a lot of ways, we all sort of understand each other, so we call it one language. The French language has an organization that decides what the correct way of communicating in French is, but the English language has never had that. We get our "correct" ways of speaking and writing mostly from our schools, which are impacted by whatever our local way of speaking is. As long as we stay in contact, this works pretty well. Sure, we talk about people having a "Southern accent," or a "Boston accent," but there's nothing in the beans of Boston that makes people talk that way. It's all about who you learn from, which is greatly influenced by the first people to speak a language in a given area. For instance, because New England was settled by people from an area of England who didn't pronounce their r's, people in Boston now "Pahk the cah in Havahd Yahd."

But what does this have to do with the military? Think back to when you first became a member of the military. This experience surrounds you with people from all over the country, based on the job you will do in the military. If you're going to be in the infantry, you'll probably do Basic and AIT all in Georgia. Do you remember all the different ways people spoke at first – and then how important was it that you had clear communication during training? The effect of this was that you had to relax some of your ways of speaking to help others understand. You couldn't just use the words you used "back on the block." You had to use words that everyone could understand.

Let me take you back to the settling of the United States again. On the East Coast, a bunch of people from different European areas settled along the Eastern Seaboard of the US, all with different ways of speaking already. But when those same people moved West, they did so all at pretty much the same time. When we think about the vast West now, we don't think of many specific accents, besides maybe "Surfer Dude," and "Valley Girl," on the extreme West Coast of California. The rest of the West seems to not have much of an accent at all. That's because it was settled basically all at once by a lot of people speaking all kinds of different dialects of English and other languages. And so, in order to accommodate communication, they changed the way they spoke slowly and subtly in order to make sure others could understand them.

Back at training, this same process happened to all of us. We slowly began to change the way we spoke at home to something more neutral and understandable, or else we got really strong doing pushups. By the end of training, the guy from New York stopped saying "son" at the end of all of his sentences. The guy from Tidewater Virginia started saying "about" instead of "aboot." And the guy from Wisconsin finally stopped referring to bagels like they were capable of carrying something.

The leveling out of the way you spoke was only the first step in learning to speak like the rest of the military. Next, you were given a book. This book was written in the South and it told you exactly how to pronounce things over the radio (in a way that sounded more or less Southern). It told you the names of all your new gear. It told you the names of the structure of your leadership and introduced you to concepts you'd never thought about.

For us Army guys, it was TRADOC 600-4, the soldier's Blue Book. We learned this book inside and out. We memorized large sections of it. We recited it on pain of pushups. Promotion boards later tested us on it. It was our constant companion and our only guide to whatever the drill sergeant had just said.

When I conducted research on this collection of words for my doctoral program, I found that my participants had no less than 60% recall ability on them, no matter how long they had been out of the military. When I asked civilians about these words, most of them had no clue what I was talking about unless they had a military spouse or family member, and even then, they didn't know exactly what each one meant. So, not only did you change the way you spoke from the people back home for the course of your training so that you could more easily be understood, but you also learned hundreds of new words and concepts to describe the things you were doing.

In addition to the dialect levelling and the book, the drill sergeants spoke in a way that modeled a new grammatical structure. Position of attention, move! Back home, do you ever recall anyone saying, "Downstairs...Let's go!" I mean, besides maybe Yoda, nobody talks like this outside of the military, but God help you if you fail to understand what the drill sergeant is telling you.

The drill sergeants use this grammatical structure in conjunction with the new vocabulary you learn from your book and the new way of pronouncing words found in the radio operator's handbook, and with all of those together, the military reforms the way you speak. Have you ever had dreams in military speak? It's the same thing as when Rosetta Stone asks if you have ever dreamed in French. It's a different way of speaking -- when you dream in it, it's because you're fluent in it.

Differences in the way people speak are
born of two factors, on a single spectrum:
contact and isolation. That is to say, when I
am isolated from a specific social group, our
ways of speaking grow farther apart. When
I am in constant contact with a social group,
our ways of speaking grow closer together.
Remember the five-minute limit on your
calls in basic training? The ones that only
happened once a week, if you were lucky,
and only after red phase? Those were
isolating you from speaking the way people
spoke back home. You were being isolated
from your dialect. Isolation from your home
dialect and contact with a new exemplar
created the conditions for your transition.
Don't tune out on me because it sounds like
I'm telling you you've been brainwashed.
My guess is your drill sergeant wasn't
familiar with sociolinguistic theory. The
effect, however, remains the same.

In short, your buddy who sounds like an
idiot: you need to stop hanging out with

him because every moment you spend together, you're influencing each other's ways of speaking. While that might benefit him, eventually something's going to come out of your mouth that you would have never said before.

After training, you spend most of your time with other members of the military. You do your job, speaking with members of the military all day. Maybe you live in the barracks and you speak with members of the military during leisure too. Maybe you live on post and you have barbecues with other members of the military and their spouses. Maybe you go out after work with people from the military. When you travel, you probably go to places to which you can catch a free flight, which means you're mostly traveling to places around a military base. You isolate yourself from people who don't speak the way military people speak and you have contact primarily with people who do speak the way the military speaks.

As a consequence, you speak more and more like a member of the military. This is great for your career -- people come to see you behaving, looking, acting, sounding, and being more like a member of the military, which gets you promotions. But the more you isolate yourself from civilians, the harder it is for them to understand what you say. You still understand them, so it seems like they're just being deliberately obtuse, but you have begun to speak in a way that prevents them from understanding about every tenth word you say.

If you don't believe me, I want you to find a stranger in the next week who you know isn't a military member and tell them about BRM. Talk to them like you would any other soldier and just see what happens. They'll think you're a nut. That's because they don't have context to understand what you're talking about. Maybe they'll understand some basics about marksmanship, but will they know that for a week you walked to the range every day? Will they understand that foxholes are cold? Will they even know what a foxhole is? Will they understand why a drill sergeant would kick rounds into your hole (because they don't want to be there either)? They don't know the same words that you do. They don't have the context you have. They don't speak like people in the military speak. So, what can you do?

Self Work
Can you think of a military concept that might be difficult to explain to a civilian? What would that be and how might you go about explaining it?

_____

_____

_____

_____

_____

_____

_____

_____

_____

_____

If you're reading this book, you're probably about to leave the military, or maybe you've been out for a while and you just feel like you didn't quite get enough from your transition program. Either way, as I said above, the more you hang around with particular people, the more you each understand each other. My suggestion is to find a civilian social group to which you can belong. A good example for me is my church, which has its own way of speaking. We talk about "seasons of life" and things that people who don't go to my church don't really understand on the same level as people in the church group do. Within the church, I also have a group of friends. We share even more of the same ways of speaking. I will still occasionally slip in a word or two without knowing it, but I have made my friends aware that I do this and given them permission to ask for clarification, so they know they can do this and what to expect when it happens. It has taken me a long time to develop these skills, though. What can you do in the meantime?

Well, being in the military, I'm sure you were familiar with "fake it til you make it." That's sort of what I'm going to ask you to do here. I'm going to ask you to write down five short story ideas and I want you to write them just as you would if you were telling your buddies, maybe even the ones you lived them with.

Then we're going to look those stories over and see if we can unpack them for a civilian audience. Where are we using coded language? Where are we saying things that civilians can't understand? Where are we using an odd grammatical structure, or tripping up our readers with something surprising? Go ahead.

Self Work
What are your story ideas?

1. _____
2. _____
3. _____
4. _____
5. _____

Take some time to write a little more about one or two of these stories.

_____

_____

_____

_____

_____

_____

_____

_____

_____

_____

_____

_____

_____

_____

_____

_____

_____

_____

_____

_____
_____
_____
_____
_____
_____

What is some of the language in your
story(s) that might be coded?

_____
_____
_____
_____
_____

Are there any concepts civilians might not
understand?

_____
_____
_____
_____
_____

Is there any part where you use grammar or idioms that are unfamiliar or unexpected to civilians?

_____

_____

_____

_____

_____

If you're going through this book without a facilitator, you might be wondering what I mean. So, let's unpack this a little.

One of the most common examples of coded language is when military members introduce themselves to each other. There's a lot of information encoded into the questions you might ask another service member.

The first thing you might ask is branch of service. The branches (Army, Navy, Marines, Air Force, Coast Guard, Space

Force) tell us a lot about the conditions under which someone served. If someone served in the Air Force, chances are they had nice gear, nice barracks, good food, and their NCO's cared more about their uniforms being pressed than how fast they could run two miles. If someone served in the Marines, they don't know that blue and red clashes with black and white, and especially with tan and green! I kid, but seriously: we understand things about veterans based upon the branches in which they served. We have certain expectations, certain stereotypes, and these are all built into their identification with a particular branch of service.

Another piece of encoded information is what your Military Occupational Specialty (MOS) was. If I encounter a guy who was 11-series in the Army and still looks like he's in pretty good shape, I am not going to pick a fight with this dude. That's just not something I'm going to do, but a civilian doesn't know just from hearing that someone was an 11-B that their primary job for the last however-many-years was to train as a killer. They might just be the idiot to pick a fight with this guy, and I might just want to be a fly on the wall for that short engagement. I'm not going to go play paintball with a Ranger, and I'm not going to try to manipulate an 18-series. I'm going to trust the spreadsheets given to me by a 92-Y.

This is what I mean by encoded language. If I start a story with the words, "I was mounted with the 88M's on MRAPs on my way to the FOB 20k down the road from Camp Liberty during OIF," I have lost my civilian audience at "mounted." They don't know anything else I said. So, when we're telling our stories, if we want to be understood, we need to decode them. Instead of what I said above, I may say, "I was riding on the outside of one of our armored vehicles on the way to a smaller base from one of the big camps when I was in Iraq." I've said pretty much the same thing, but now I haven't lost my audience right at the outset.

There are many metaphorical landmines in our writing for civilian audiences. I don't expect you to eliminate all of the specialized language that makes your experience what it is. What I am saying, or writing, I guess... is that the more you can translate your story into language a civilian can understand, the better that civilian WILL understand your story and the weight that it carries. They will better understand the weight that you carry. They will begin to understand parts of how you act and move through the world that you didn't think anyone would ever understand again.

So don't make your stories inauthentic; don't eliminate your voice. Just think about who your audience is ahead of time. Think about what they can handle from you. Tell your stories. Make them fun. Make your friends understand you. It's worth it. It's so worth it, I promise you.

If you run out of stories you've translated and prepared, I encourage you to warn people that you're about to get real and then go slow, be deliberate and decode on the fly. Granted, this is only when people or a person who really wants to know you is listening. I know it can be scary. But you're not meant to do life alone.

Now go ahead. You have some stories already written down in military speak. I want you to take those stories and pick one to translate right now before you put this book down. See what it feels like.

Once you have it, go tell a close friend your story. Watch the reaction. Did you see the look of recognition? How did that feel?

Self Work
Write down your translated story here.

_____

_____

_____

_____

_____

_____

_____

_____

_____

_____

_____

_____

_____

_____

_____

_____

_____

_____

_____

Step 3: Our spectrum from the worst day to the best day is totally out of sync with the rest of the world. We need to learn that 0% and 100% feels the same for everyone.

I was listening to a fellow vet speak one day at the writing program I ran in Fargo. He was speaking about the Battle of Iwo Jima. He had been on one of the assault crafts that eventually stormed the beach and took the island. When I say *had been*, I mean he got off.

Before the craft went to the beach, the craft that held all his friends, he was pulled off the craft because of a bruise on his thigh. He watched the naval battery fire from the deck of a ship as his buddies landed and were cut to pieces by machine gun fire. You want to talk about survivor's guilt? This guy was literally snatched from the jaws of death by a bruise on his thigh. Imagine all of the days in your life. Imagine the worst possible day. Imagine being this guy. That feeling in the pit of your stomach: that's the same feeling he felt. Maybe you think the depths of sorrow he must have sunk to were certainly more intense than anything you have ever felt, but I want you to come along with me here: our worst day feels the same as everyone else's worst day.

We've all looked at someone else in pain and scoffed. Maybe it's a child crying over the passing of a pet. Maybe it's someone who has just missed a deadline. Maybe there's a relationship has ended. We naturally feel like we need to place a value on people's pain and compare it to our own before deciding how much empathy to show. At least, that was always the case for me. It was easy to look at someone else in pain and decide that it wasn't enough to warrant the reaction they were having, and they needed to toughen up. This can be especially true for veterans, who, on the whole, experience ridiculous amounts of stress that civilians will, for the most part, never have to face. Even the most stressful civilian jobs don't usually deal with life and death on a daily basis. Many military jobs do, though. From parachute riggers to submarine engineers, from cooks to Predator sensor operators, people in the military deal with life and death on a totally inordinate number of their days.

Is it any wonder then that veterans leave the service and view the day-to-day problems of civilians as trivial? We see people break down and lose their minds over what seems like the smallest thing, and we scoff. But I'm here to tell you: no amount of scoffing is going to heal your pain. No amount of callousness toward civilians will ever be enough for you to feel as good as you often felt in the military. At some point, someone somewhere is going to need you to have empathy for them and, frankly, if you haven't done some work on yourself, that's not going to happen. You won't be capable. And when we're not capable of empathy, a whole rash of other things can go wrong.

So, what is this self-work I speak of? You have to start from the assumption that everyone's worst day and best day feel the same. Everyone has the same capacity for physical responses to emotions. If something brings me to tears, no matter what that thing is, the tears feel the same.

I now want you to write down what happened on your worst day. You don't have to show this to anyone. Don't dwell on it too much. Just think about what happened on your worst day, and write it down.

Self Work
What happened on your worst day?

_____
_____
_____
_____
_____
_____
_____

Now, I want you to write down what
happened on your best day. Take a moment
to describe what made it your best day.
What was the weather like? What could you
smell? Who was there with you? Was it a
religious experience? Did it feel
supernatural? Go ahead.

Self Work

What happened on your best day?

_____

_____

_____

_____

_____

_____

_____

_____

_____

Now with your worst day on one end of the line and your best day on the other end of the line, I want you to fill in a few more days. Just write a short prompt for each one to fill in the line. It might be easiest to start with one of the days you were most bored or one that felt really normal.

0%   50%   100%

What you've created is your spectrum from your worst day to your best. 0% is your worst day and 100% is your best. Everyone who does this exercise with me has a 0% and 100%. There are no exceptions. Each person describes emotions like hopelessness and pain at 0%. Each person describes emotions like joy and pride at 100%. Each person feels the same about their 0% and 100%. This is because we don't know what will come later or how we will respond, and so we react with 100% of our positive emotion each time we experience a new best day. Each time we experience a new worst day, we respond with 0% of our positive emotion. That's just the way we're wired. Whatever you're capable of feeling on those days, you will.

I've said all this to say: our spectra are all messed up. Civilians haven't had the experiences we've had. Even just after you arrived at basic training, you experienced abuse that few people will ever have directed at them.

We talk about making sacrifices for the good of our country; this is one of those sacrifices. We don't get to hold ourselves above civilians because we have experienced what we consider to be greater pain. We sacrificed for our country in order to prevent people from experiencing that greater pain. We are the sheep dogs guarding the flock. We are the penguins on the outside of the huddle, blocking the wind. We are the linemen who protect the quarterback.

Yes, you're going to experience a broader spectrum of emotions in your life by virtue of how messed up your worst day probably was. But until we experience those extremes, our pain doesn't feel different for not having experienced them. Do not cheapen your sacrifice. Show the love for others that you showed when you took your oath. Do not belittle the pain of others. Take pride in having guarded them from pain they might not have been able to take.

The problem with pain is that it makes us feel isolated, like nobody has ever felt like we do in this moment. When I was in the Army, I couldn't fathom how God could let pain like mine exist. I liked to ask my Christian friends what, for instance, the point of childhood bone cancer was.

C.S. Lewis' *The Problem of Pain* gives us a kind of answer: pain exists in order to help us love one another. I paraphrase, but essentially, if there were no problems, no pain, what would there be to feel empathy about?

Because we have free will, we exist in a natural world; pain cannot be stricken from the natural world because it is real. The struggle for survival is real. Good and evil are real. Pain is real. And the fact that all these things are real means we all experience them together. We aren't alone in our pain. Everyone in the world experiences pain, and ours is no different.

Our 100% is equal to everyone else's 100%. In short, you're not the only special snowflake in the world with pain, buddy.

I don't mean to belittle what you've been through. I know it was hard. But I do mean to keep you from belittling the pain of others as you transition back to the life you fought to afford people, the life that was promised to you as a result of your service. Rejoice in the pain of dog poop on the carpet. Delight in the pain of spilled coffee. Thank God for the pain of injury-free fender benders. As my buddy Ajax would say, nobody is getting shot at around here today.

Self Work

I'm going to ask you to write something
difficult here. Think back to a time when
someone's pain sounded trivial to you. This
could be a friend, a child, a spouse, or
anyone with whom you've interacted.

What were they going through?

_____
_____
_____
_____
_____
_____

How did they react to going through that?

_____
_____
_____
_____
_____

How did you react when they told you or showed you?

_____

_____

_____

_____

_____

How did your reaction make them feel?

_____

_____

_____

_____

Is that what you wanted?

_____

_____

_____

Step 4: Know your skills and plan to explain how they're an asset. Not everyone knows why you laugh when someone asks the stress question.

In the late nineties, Army recruiting put out a commercial featuring paratroopers jumping out of an aircraft ramp. The narrator said, "Some day, a job interviewer is going to ask how you handle stressful situations. Try not to laugh." I remembered this question when I got out of the Army, and found that I was indeed asked it, and I indeed had to keep from laughing. (Laughing at this question doesn't help you get jobs, by the way. The interviewer just comes away thinking you're nuts.)

There is a very real difference between the way some interview questions hit veterans and civilians. Maybe they'll ask you the stress question or maybe they'll ask about conflict resolution, or or maybe they'll ask the big one: "Describe your worst day at work."

Remember back in Step 2, where we talked about having party stories? You need to have interview stories too. They can be the same stories, but they still need to be translated, and you will need to ask yourself a question with each one: "How much trauma do I inflict on this interviewer today?" It's important that you have a plan for some of these questions because, chances are, you're the only veteran they're interviewing today. Your responses can either help you stand out or make you look like a huge weirdo.

Self Work

Have you ever been asked questions like
those listed above in a job interview or
similar situation?

_____

_____

_____

_____

How did those questions make you feel?

_____

_____

_____

_____

_____

_____

_____

_____

How did you respond?

_____

_____

_____

_____

_____

_____

_____

You haven't yet heard me decry any of this as unjust or unfair. I know that you all have recognized your sacrifices from the beginning. Perhaps you're resistant to saying anything is unfair -- you feel like you did a job, got paid, and finished. Well, let me tell you, this part is probably the sneakiest actually-unfair aspect of having served in the military. Nobody else gets asked the stress question and has to summon up a story that won't inflict mental anguish on the interviewer. Nobody else has to consider whether or not the information that they relate about their worst day might contain details that could get them thrown into lockup at Fort Leavenworth. This is your burden to bear and it sucks. Civilians don't have those experiences, so it's hard for them to fathom a response that might be traumatizing for an interviewer. They think back to a day when the printer broke or someone spilled coffee or an animal got into the office. You have to wonder if the interviewer can handle the story about picking up body parts and throwing them in a cargo net.

Instead of just lingering in frustration about how unfair it is, though, we can make a plan. There are tons of lists of commonly-asked interview questions online. You can look at these and prepare a response for each one. Ask a friend if your response seems reasonable. Pick someone who knows some of your party stories. Ask if one of those might be more applicable. If you're at a college, chances are they have a career office that may offer interview practice. Take them up on it. Do those practice interviews. Lean on friends you can trust. Find your local Veteran Service Office and ask if they might also have some kind of help. Ask at your church or community center. You don't have to be ashamed of needing help. We all need help, and we weren't meant to do life alone.

Self Work

Use some of the questions below and make a plan about what to say.

1. Have you ever failed at something important?

_____
_____
_____

2. How do you handle stress?

_____
_____
_____
_____

3. Have you ever been a part of a team?

_____
_____
_____
_____

4. What would a previous co-worker say was an area where you needed improvement?

_____

_____

_____

5. Describe a disagreement you had with a co-worker.

_____

_____

_____

_____

6. What was your hardest day at your previous job?

_____

_____

_____

_____

_____

I don't necessarily want to make this chapter only about getting a job. It's important for us to feel valued in our communities. Nothing is more frustrating as a veteran than being told how to do something you already know how to do, especially when you learned it under extreme circumstances. What I'm trying to do is to help you communicate to everyone that you have valuable skills that can be of use in a variety of different contexts. Even though job applications are one of the easiest ways to explain these ways of thinking about your personal qualifications, I want you to feel free to use the same techniques in your personal life.

Again, part of what makes communicating with other veterans easy is that you have a code that delivers a lot of information in very few words. You say, "I served at Ft. Lewis," and your fellow veteran infers that you may be familiar with woodland combat, light mechanized infantry like Strikers, and that you probably have some idea how to survive in a mountain environment. It also communicates that you were viewed as a good enough asset to the military for them to appease you with a nice garrison assignment. Part of what makes communication with civilians harder is that this code, if one exists, isn't as obvious. Maybe you have some similar social experience or maybe you don't. You don't know, going in, which code to use. You can look at what they're wearing and make some guesses. You can listen intently for a while and see if you detect a detail that might lead you to some assumptions, but you don't necessarily know how to talk with this person right off the bat.

With that in mind, step one is: you need to find some social context that you share and hang onto that. Identify with something they say. Show them you know something about it. It doesn't need to have anything to do with the job or topic -- you're not communicating your skills at this point. What you are doing is communicating a shared context and your ability to pick up on social cues that are necessary to relate with other people on a team.

You know how to do this. You did it in Basic. There's nobody yelling this time, but you can still do it.

Once you have that shared social context, hold onto it. It's your lifeline for this conversation. If you both like *Breakfast at Tiffany's*, you've got that, and then you can move forward.

Self Work

What are some social or cultural groups
(gamers, Republicans, Christians, Hikers,
Hunters, etc) to which you belong that you
might be able to use as a point of relation
with someone?

_____

_____

_____

_____

_____

Step two in the interview process: you need
to know how to explain some of the things
you did as a job. For instance, I could say I
did manual labor under the supervision of a
middle and senior manager, and sound like I
was a mere peon. I could alternatively say,
"I maintained, issued, received, and
prepared life-saving equipment on a small
team in coordination with elite commando
units whose operating budget was
unlimited, and whose demands on my time

were high." You can see how one sounds better than the other, right? I'm sure you don't need me to tell you that you're going to have to dig a little deeper than "I was eleven bang-bang." You will need your unit, your dates of service, and your MOS identified, just in case people might know what that means, and you should then be prepared to tell people exactly what you did. Nobody spends their entire military career on the range. Talk about what filled your days. Talk about who you managed. Talk about tasks you accomplished. Talk about awards you won and why. (You and I know that everyone got the National Defense Medal from 9/11 onward, though not everyone does.) It's okay to talk about awards you really do have. Be honest. Don't try to deceive people. Don't try to say you were more than you were, but certainly make it clear all that you did.

Self Work
Describe your MOS and other work you did
in the military in words your mom would
understand.

_____

_____

_____

_____

_____

_____

_____

_____

_____

Step three: relate these experiences to
civilian jobs.

Civilian parachute riggers make bank. If I
had gone straight to civilian parachute
rigging as soon as I got out of the military, I
probably would have had a much more

interesting life. I didn't, because I spent most of my time trying to fight what I had become in the military.

I had entered as a tender-hearted artist and emerged as a hard-hearted cog in a machine. Yes, I wanted to do my patriotic duty but I wasn't bound up in toxic patriotism. I didn't think that being American made me better than everyone else. I hated that the Army made it easier for me to hate other people. I hated that I could see the expeditious, prudent action before the sympathetic, genuine action. I didn't want to be known as brutal, harsh, angry, damaged, or any of the things I thought people would think of me if I continued.

It's okay if the military didn't end up making you who you wanted to be or getting you closer to where you wanted to end up. But even if your MOS was tangentially related to where you want to be, I encourage you to relate away. For example, when I applied to be a resident advisor on my college campus, I talked about having pulled barracks duty as an E-4. I talked about doing rounds, sitting at the desk, and answering phones. I really unpacked everything that one does on barracks rounds. It was very similar to what I ended up doing as an RA. Because I had that experience in the Army, even though it had nothing to do with my job, I was able to parlay that into a level of experience valuable to the position I was applying for. The wealth of experiences you have in the military are a veritable gold mine, and you can keep coming back to it each time you interview.

But, what if you're not sure how to relate these experiences to your civilian job of choice? Well, here's a systematic way to break it down.

Check out the required qualifications in a job listing. Make sure you have a way to explain how you possess all of those things. Don't just list your unit or duty station and expect that people will know what went on there: you have to list it and be prepared to talk about how you meet each of those minimum qualifications.

Next, look at the preferred qualifications. After you're sure you meet all of the minimums, make sure you have at least some of the preferred ones covered also. In doing this, you'll make yourself a more attractive candidate on top of all of the intangibles they're already getting with a veteran.

Lastly, make sure that if there is a license required to do a specific thing and you don't have that license, you're up front about how you plan to address that. Talk about what it takes to get the license, what you've done to get it, and what experience you have without the license. I had a license to drive every wheeled vehicle in the motor pool, but do you think that meant I could get a CDL when I got out? Nope. Once, I applied for a job in a college copier machine shop. The people working in that position just ran files through a high-speed copier all day long, so I figured it would be pretty obvious that I suited the qualifications – for one, I already had a Master's degree. However, I didn't list on my resumé under *Skills* that I had experience with high-speed copiers, so my application wasn't even reviewed by a person because the machine didn't read me as qualified. Don't be me. Look at that listing. Make sure a Private could see how you were qualified to do the job. That may, in fact, be who's checking.

Self Work
Make a list of some of your skills and where
you got them.

1.

2.

3.

4.

5.

6.

7.

Fourth, and finally: be your own advocate.
You did more than just fight bad guys when
you were in the military: you adapted to
each new situation, overcame obstacles as
part of a team, you mastered all of the skills
necessary to do your job in the minimum

required time, as described by a bureaucrat. If there's something you know how to do that's not clear in the application or resumé or cover letter, let someone know. Speak up if you think there's something the company is doing that they could use your help with. In your life after the military, it's okay to tell people you're good at something. It's okay to speak up and say with confidence you can do something. Purely as a result of your willingness to speak up, you may find doors will open.

Chances are, the military way of doing things is going to be different from the ways that other people do things. That's okay. In fact, if the company hasn't had input from a veteran before, you might just revolutionize their business. But that will only happen if you speak up when you know something.

In Tom Wolfe's book, *The Right Stuff,* the author describes a kind of speech specific to the World War II-era Army. He writes, "In the Army one was continually around people who spoke Army Creole, a language in which there were about ten nouns, five verbs, and one adjective, or participle, or whatever it was called." The silence of a soldier, the stoicism, is a part of the Army dialect that Wolfe calls a Creole. It can be really difficult for us to understand that part. The way we don't speak is as much a part of the dialect as the way we do speak. So, when you find yourself clamming up about important information, it's important to ask yourself if your silence is necessary, why it's necessary, and what would change if you weren't silent.

Self Work

With these things in mind, rewrite your plans for how to answer the questions I asked.

1. Have you ever failed at something important?

_____
_____
_____

2. How do you handle stress?

_____
_____
_____
_____

3. Have you ever been a part of a team?

_____
_____
_____
_____

4. What would a previous co-worker say was an area where you needed improvement?

_____

_____

_____

5. Describe a disagreement you had with a co-worker.

_____

_____

_____

_____

6. What was your hardest day at your previous job?

_____

_____

_____

_____

_____

I've used the job metaphor in this chapter because it's a really easy one to wrap your head around; however, you can follow these steps in personal relationships too. Finding shared social context is a great way to relate to people you're finding it hard to relate to. Explaining what you did in the military in ways people can understand is a great way to satisfy curiosities about your service and let people know what it's like to serve. Relating your military jobs to civilian jobs can be a great way to illustrate these similarities and explain why you do things the way you do them. And being your own advocate can make it clear who you used to be and who you want to be in the future.

Only you can make sense of the trajectory your life has taken. Only you know what thought process led you from point A to point B. Did it make sense when you went from being Military Intelligence to working at McDonald's? Who knows. Maybe you needed a job that very day. Maybe you needed to eat while you begged Boeing for a job. Only you can explain those things. So be your own advocate and help people get to know who you are and what your skills are, what the synthesis of them says about where you are now and who you will be in the future.

Step 5: Decide who you're going to be from now on and be the best at it. Let your service feed it but make no mistake, this is a new life.

If you're reading this book, chances are your military career is over. Whatever you did is what you've done, and you're probably not going to get the chance to do much more. It's also pretty likely that being in the military has had some kind of effect on who you are.

Where you go from here can be a really big question to answer. Honestly, as hard as it might be to hear, it sort of helps if you're single and you've got the ability to start over in a new community. If you're coupled and you're going back into your existing community, there will be a much rougher transition if you let it be, unless you've got some great support. One thing is certain. As much as there was a life before the military compared to now, there's also a life after the military, compared to now. They are not the same.

You see, in the time when we joined, we expected that we were leaving a relatively stable community. The changes over the years had mostly been predictable to us -- we were living within the community and we were a part of the goings-on in the community. But when we interrupted that stream to step out of the community and into the military community, all of the sudden we were representatives of that community, yet apart from the community. We stepped out of the ability to perceive the changes as they were taking place and stepped into a community isolated from that community of origin.

When we return, we expect that we are coming back to our community as we left it, but in reality, we are coming back to a very different place. The longer we've been away, the more the place is likely to have changed. We expected to return home, but in reality, the home we left will never exist again, just like the person we were before the military will never exist again.

We can of course become bitter about how the world didn't throw us a parade. We can instead use who we are now in what the community is now and create something better.

One of the first communities I attempted to rejoin after the military was Browns Valley, MN. I worked for one of the only local companies in this tiny little town and made it a point to insert myself into community and political affairs. I found that the community was starting a local chapter of the Lion's Club and was looking for officers to help lead the chapter. I joined and found that most of the leadership were stuck in using the same old funding methods for community projects. I brought a philosophy from my Army unit of using what the community had available that made it unique, thus making that the focus of its fundraising. Everyone seemed to like this idea, so we settled on a rubber duck race as our first fundraiser. We bought and numbered ducks and allowed the community to purchase ducks to win prizes. The balance of the race proceeds would go toward building new playground equipment at the school. We used the unique geographic feature of the local river, the existing culture of active gamblers, and the shared interest in keeping the local school nice as a way to bring the community together around the common goals set forth in the project. Now Browns Valley has held several annual duck races, put on by the local chapter of the Lions.

You can be an asset to your community because of your very status as someone who has existed outside of the community. You bring fresh ideas. You bring new insights. You have seen how things get done and know how to get them done. You know how teams work. You know what works and what doesn't and you know how to scale things from small to large and back again. You aren't blind to the assets that have always been in the community; you can see weaknesses and strengths that others might blindly accept as fact. These are not small or insignificant qualities. These are exactly what some communities need in order to succeed.

Self Work

Who are you now? What qualities/assets do you have? How could you leverage these to help a community or group?

_____

_____

_____

_____

_____

_____

_____

What are the strengths and weaknesses in your community? What are its assets?

_____

_____

_____

_____

_____

_____

_____

_____

_____

_____

_____

_____

_____

_____

_____

_____

_____

How can you use this knowledge to
continue your mission to make people
happier, safer, and freer?

_____

_____

_____

_____

_____

_____

_____

_____

_____

_____

_____

_____

_____

_____

_____

_____

Let me tell you another story. This one is a little older.

There was a strong young lady who left her community to join the Marines. She was a high-speed, low-drag Marine. She could keep up with any other Marine. She won award after award. She was decorated time and again. She even led other Marines in combat. She rose high in the ranks and retired young, with her honor intact.

When she came home, she had a few good friends who threw her a party. She had a little family, and everything was in place for her to just relax her way to a long life.

This Marine had enough structure in place that she didn't feel like she needed to work at integrating with her community. She didn't feel the need to explain herself. If someone didn't respect her service, they weren't worth her time.

She took this attitude to every function: every PTA meeting at the kids' school, every work meeting at her new job, and every community group she participated in. When people asked her to talk about her service, she stayed quiet. When people asked her to do something she thought was beneath her, she didn't give her full effort. When someone complained about a problem in their life, she belittled them for their weakness.

At some point she felt like the school board was not spending its time and budget wisely and decided to run for president of it. She ran on a platform of being an NCO who could reform the processes of the board and clean up its priorities. But when it came time to talk about her qualifications to the public, she could only speak about her skills in abstractions. She couldn't tell people what really happened during her service because she knew they wouldn't understand.

Because she couldn't talk about these things and didn't know a way to make her qualifications clear, not only was she not elected, but other people running for the office defined her service for her. They accused her of war crimes. They accused her of being too masculine. They told people she wasn't mentally stable. She became shunned in her community. Even her husband, who had been emasculated by the accusations, left her; because of the rumors about her in the community, he was granted custody of the children.

A few years later, she got back with an old boyfriend (a fellow veteran) and decided to run for school board again. She wanted to maintain a presence in the kids' life. She wanted to set the record of her service straight.

This time she was brutally honest when her opponents attacked her. She talked about every detail of her service and crushed her opponents in the race. She won the position and was elected school board president.

But when she was finally seated on the school board, the other board members were afraid of her. Those things that had been an asset in the race because of her authenticity were now out in the open, and the other board members were too fearful to oppose her. Every reform she instituted was passed unanimously, and things got a little better, but after a while, she couldn't stand the spinelessness of the board members and she quit.

By this time, she had been out of the Marines for ten years. She was just over 50 years old and was no closer to having the kind of community outside the military that she had always wanted. Meanwhile, the old boyfriend had become the new husband and he had issues of his own. She was unable to get custody of the kids, who by this time were close to grown up anyway. There was a trail of collateral damage left in her wake. She had cheapened her sacrifice for her country and was no more loved than when she first enlisted.

I've seen so many of my sisters and brothers with versions of the same story, and it isn't new. It happened to Ajax after the Trojan War. It happened to Coriolanus in Rome. It happened to Henry the Fifth after Agincourt. The experience of not being able to come home is an age-old story that has been recorded as a problem in cultures as long as there have been cultures with veterans in them. It will continue to be a problem even if everyone who ever leaves the military reads this book.

There is no right answer that will bring everyone home. Some of us will never get there. For some of us, we don't know what home looks like anymore. For some of us, we have to define home all over again.

It's going to take work. It's not easy work. But you can take the first steps right now.

I want you to write down a few things for me.

Self Work

Write down what home used to be like.

_____
_____
_____
_____
_____
_____
_____
_____
_____
_____
_____

Think about what has changed about you
and what parts of your home you think you
could bring back.

_____

_____

_____

_____

_____

Write down the parts of home that will
never be back.

_____

_____

_____

_____

_____

_____

_____

_____

_____

Now that you have a clear picture of what home used to be, what it can be in the future, and what it will never be again, I want you to write down a detailed plan for the first year post-military, a less-detailed plan for the first five years after the military, and then some goals for 10 and 20 years after the military. These goals should build on each other to achieve what home could be. If you've been out for awhile, I want you to plan from now onward, armed with the knowledge you now have, how things might change moving forward.

While you're doing this, dream big. Big dreams can seem impossible, but putting them out there, even if they're way down-range, can make it easier to aim yourself in the right direction.

Self Work

My plan for my first year post-military:

I will live in:

_____

_____

I will work at:

_____

_____

_____

I will drive:

_____

_____

_____

I will work toward:

_____

_____

_____

_____

_____

_____

_____

_____

I will learn:

_____

_____

_____

_____

_____

_____

_____

_____

Or else:

_____

_____

_____

_____

_____

_____

I will rely on these five people:

_____

_____

_____

_____

_____

I will connect with my community by:

_____

_____

_____

_____

_____

_____

In the first five years post-military, I will:

_____

_____

_____

_____

_____

_____

_____

_____

_____

_____

In my first ten years post-military, I will:

_____

_____

_____

_____

_____

_____

_____

_____

_____

_____

In my first 20 years post-military, I will:

_____
_____
_____
_____
_____
_____
_____
_____
_____

A dream for my life that seems impossible right now is:

_____
_____
_____
_____
_____
_____
_____
_____
_____
_____

I do not have all of the answers you will need, but I hope you've come away with some useful insights. And I hope that your fundamental takeaway is this: the absolute best way to make it after you leave the military is to do life in fellowship with other people.

Just like the Army of One slogan doesn't make a bit of sense, doing life alone doesn't make a bit of sense. You have friends and family for a reason; you need them in order to survive.

Maybe that's a tough sell. Maybe you burned some bridges on your way down range -- I know I did. Recover what you can and drive on. Build new what can't be repaired. Lean on people, on God, and on those safety nets that were designed for you.

Do not be ashamed to go get a free meal on Veteran's Day. Go to the VA.

Take care of yourself. You deserve it.

Welcome home.

Made in the USA
Monee, IL
15 January 2023

25329640R10079